SPIRIT OF THE WIND

A photographic celebration of the wild horses of the Namib Desert

Published by
Medina Publishing Ltd
310 Ewell Road
Surbiton
Surrey KT6 7AL
United Kingdom
www.medinapublishing.com

Designed by Kitty Carruthers & Miona Janeke
Printed and bound by Toppan Leefung Printers Ltd, China

ISBN: 978-1-909339-33-0

CIP Data: A catalogue record for this book is available from the British Library.

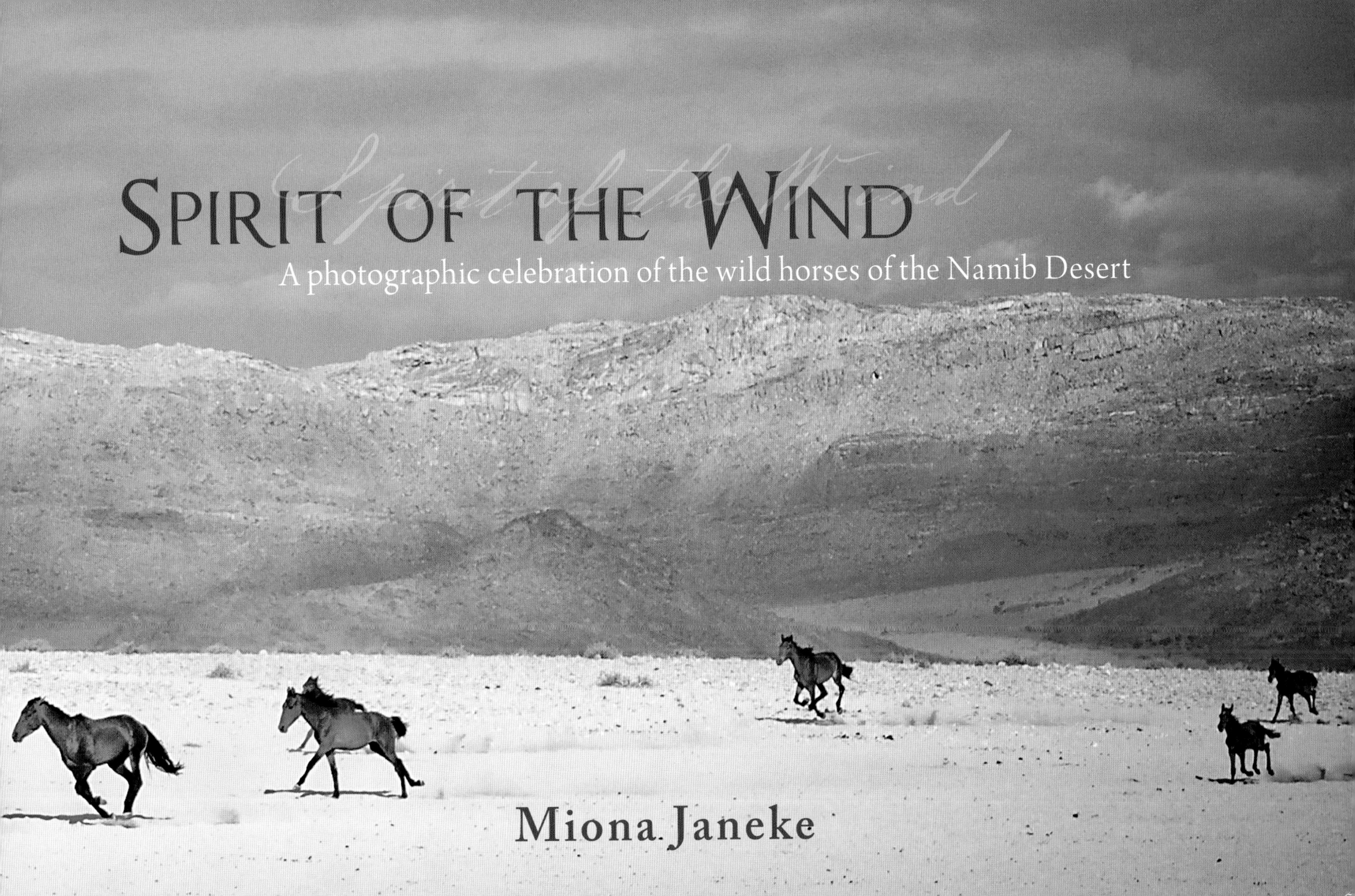

SPIRIT OF THE WIND

A photographic celebration of the wild horses of the Namib Desert

Miona Janeke

Dedicated to my grandparents, Christo and Lena, and

my mother Paula, who ignited the spark.

ACKNOWLEDGEMENTS

As I look back on my journey – from girlhood with my Grandpa on our farm, the early years of exhibiting as a photographer, my time in the desert with the horses and right up to the present – I realise how many people have helped and encouraged me along the way. So many times over the years, just when I felt like giving up the idea of a book, fate took a hand and the right people crossed my path. Without them, this book would never have been published, and I am grateful to be able to thank those who made it possible.

My Grandpa Christo Mann, who opened my eyes to the beauty of horses; my mother Paula (Mann) Huysamer, who always believed in me; and my family, who tried their best to understand my lifelong love of horses;
Mannfred Goldbeck for sharing his profound knowledge of the horses, for taking an interest in this book and for writing the Foreword;
Mannfred, with Thelanie Greyling and Ron Swilling – thank you for sharing your insights into the wild horses of the Namib Desert in your excellent publications;
Sharifa Sarra Ghazi Nasser of the Hashemite royal family, who believed in me enough to introduce me to Kitty Carruthers;
Kitty and the team at Medina Publishing in London– working with you has been a privilege;
Denis Beckett for your help with contacts; Naas Steenkamp for editing and Martin Lubikowski for drawing the map;
The Swiegers family of Klein-Aus Vista Lodge – I'll never forget the treat of a good coffee on the veranda;
Paul van Schalkwyk (may he rest in peace), Joe Gross, Tony Figuera and Pompie Burger – four Namibian photographers who have given me inspiration and been kind to me;
Lanie Dreyer Steyn from the Frameshop in Windhoek; Rynand Mudge and his family for my stay in Windhoek.
The many friends who encouraged me – too many to name, but you know who you are and I hope that you realise what you mean to me.

To all of you, thank you.
It has been an unforgettable journey.

ANGOLA

Cunene
Namacunde
Cuangar
Okavango

Opuwa

ETOSHA
NATIONAL
PARK

*Etosha
Pan*

Okaukuejo

MANGETTI
NATIONAL
PARK

KHAUDUM
NATIONAL
PARK

ZAMBIA

Luiana   Sesheke
                    Livingstone
            Kasane
            Victoria
            Falls

Zambezi

C a p r i v i   S t r i p

Harare

ZIMBABWE

Bulawayo

Grootfontein

Skeleton Coast

SKELETON COAST PARK

N A M I B

Otjiwarongo

WATERBERG
PLATEAU
PARK

Brandberg
The Spitzkoppe
Omaruru
Usakos   Karibib

Maun

Orapa

*Atlantic
Ocean*

N

Swakopmund
Walvis Bay

NAMIB DESERT

WINDHOEK   Gobabis

Rehoboth

NAMIB NAUKLUFT PARK

NAMIBIA

Ghanzi

B O T S W A N A

*K A L A H A R I
D E S E R T*

Mariental

Gaborone

Garub
Lüderitz   Aus
        GONDWANA
        DESERT COLLECTION
        KLEIN-AUS VISTA

SPERRGEBIET NATIONAL PARK

Keetmanshoop

HOT SPRINGS
& FISH RIVER
CANYON PARK

Karasburg

Alexander Bay
Port Nolloth

Orange

SOUTH AFRICA

Upington

THE WILD HORSES OF THE
NAMIB DESERT

0   100   200   300   400   500 kilometres

5

Introduction

BY MANNFRED GOLDBECK

After a century of freedom, the wild horses of the Namib Desert have become an integral part of the country and one of the top tourist attractions, epitomising the deep and glowing qualities of Namibia, the wild and rugged freedom that is found in the endless swathes of desert, craggy outcrops and inselbergs, and forever landscapes.

Like Namibia's multi-faceted population, the horses came from elsewhere and made their home in the south-western corner of Africa. Abandoned at a tumultuous time in history during World War I, they gradually made their way from the Kubub stud farm to the Garub waterhole, joining up with horses that were abandoned when the Union of South Africa troops pursued their German foes. From then on, they did what horses know best, and what is ingrained in their genes after aeons of evolution in fluctuating environments - they adapted and they survived.

The Namib horses give us the rare opportunity to view the behaviour of horses in the wild. Horses were first domesticated 5000 to 6000 years ago by nomadic people of the Eurasian steppes. They have been in service to humankind ever since for the advancement of civilisation; for conquest, agriculture and industry, sport and recreation. The wild horse populations that are dotted around the globe today, with the exception of the Przewalski's Horse, all originated from domestic stock. There is a raw and special beauty seeing how these grand animals remembered their innate nature and calling, reclaimed their freedom and returned seamlessly to their ancient ways in the desert wilderness.

Protected for many years by the borders of the Sperrgebiet, the forbidden diamond mining area, the wild horses now reside in the Namib Naukluft Park. Extensive research has shown that they do not compete with or displace the indigenous wildlife, and that they have found a niche in the desert environment.

Watching family groups at the Garub waterhole and the natural dynamics of the horses is a powerful and awe-inspiring experience, as is watching them gallop in to quench their thirst, their manes flying in the wind and the dust exploding in clouds around their hooves in the energy and excitement of the moment. It's a sight that stirs the soul, touches us in the unfathomable depths of our beings, settles somewhere close to the heart and remains there.

The Namibs' lives are not easy, luxurious or comfortable, shaped by the rainfall and seasons in the harsh Namib Desert and tempered by the cycle of life and death in the wild, but their spirit is indomitable.

Like their home, this country of space and soul, Namibia, their unfettered wild spirit and freedom nurtures dreams, inspires venture and voyages – and integrity. And always, always, calls you to return.

Namibia offers the superlative chance to rediscover freedom and peace away from the clutter and hustle-and-bustle of civilisation, to go on soul-searching journeys, like Miona's, and to fill your life with inspiration and life-affirming promise. We celebrate the spirit of the wind with her, and the essence of the wild horses which she has captured so gracefully in her photographs.

Mannfred Goldbeck
Co-author of *Wild Horses in the Namib Desert: An equine biography*

Where it all started

I went on a journey. Solo. Bought a pick-up truck (a bakkie, as we call it in South Africa), packed my camping gear, and set off on an impulse that I did not myself fully understand. I just knew that I had to go. As I set my sights on the arid reaches of the country north of Cape Town, I felt the powerful tug of a place far away where wild horses roam.

Days later, far beyond the Great River, I stopped. I had driven 2,000 kilometres on my own, through ever-bleaker desolation. Here, I thought, my dream will be realised.

I stared over the nothingness. Mirages danced in the distance. A dust devil stood on its tail nearby. I turned off the engine, and with it the air-conditioning that I had had the sense to have installed. I looked left, then right, then straight ahead again. I opened the door to a blast of scorching air and the emptiness all round. I realised that I had never been truly alone until that moment. What was I thinking? No cell phone reception! No radio reception! My adventure had begun...

The air burned my face as I set foot on the hard-baked sand. Yes, over there! That must be the waterhole; I would find them there, I was told. And I had timed it perfectly to arrive in the late afternoon when the light would be at its best and the moment was right for equine thirst to be quenched – so I was told. I stood in the blazing heat. There was no shade to be seen anywhere, all the way to the horizon, just sand, dust and endless expanse . . . except for a tiny corrugated iron shack, incongruous in the emptiness. There, on a rusted old drum, sat a man who stared disinterestedly past me.

"Is this where the horses come?", I asked. "When did you last see them?" He slowly shook his head, and that was that.

Somewhat deflated, I walked down to the man-made watering place so I could at least tell the folks back home that I had been there, seen it, seen their tracks, even if I had nothing else to show for it. A bit like Peter Matthiesen and his vain quest through the Hindu Kush in search of the elusive snow leopard. He never found it but wrote a wonderful book, *The Snow Leopard*, about the importance of the quest. Sometimes, he agrees, "'tis a better thing to travel hopefully than to arrive".

I sat on the cement slab and stared toward the horizon, intensely aware of the silence pressing in on me. How many people on the planet have ever experienced utter, deafening silence? I kicked up some dust to check my hearing. The sound was grating, intrusive. I could hear my own breathing. But slowly, in a chain of measured heartbeats, I sensed myself becoming transfixed by the implacable desolation around me. A fleeting feeling of bliss and wonderment passed through me. Is this what the ancient man at the shack feels like every day? Or ever?
Then came the sense of awe. A distant rumbling had me scanning the empty skies. Thunder with not a cloud in the sky? It grew louder, the ground began to tremble. I peered into the heatwaves trembling towards me from the horizon, creating images that morphed into liquid galloping horses. The pounding of hooves came nearer, and a cloud of golden dust rose in the light of the setting sun. The liquid forms solidified into the surreal silhouettes of horses running full-tilt for water.

A hundred metres short of the waterhole they slowed to a halt. Ears pitched forward, some with muzzles to the ground and others sniffing the air, they apprehensively checked me out. With the sun in my eyes I dared not blink, not wanting to miss a movement. As the dust settled I snapped out of my daze and realized that I was what was stopping them from their water. I backed away slowly and, as they cautiously passed, I saw the thirst in their eyes and the burning will to survive. They lowered their heads, some keeping a wary eye on me. Sucking up the cool water in long gulps, they quenched their thirst.

I turned to smile at the man by the shack to share this special moment with somebody, anybody, but he was nowhere – he had vanished. I wondered if he been a mirage too, conjured by my mind to contend with the silence and isolation of the desert?

In the middle of nowhere was a tiny shack, but as to the whereabouts of the horses, there was no telling. It was not until I found this photograph recently that I realised the encounter had not been a figment of my imagination.

The picture opposite is one of my favourite images because it reminds me of the sublime serenity of the moment. As the sun rose ove the dunes, the colours took my breath away.

So there I stood, nursing my happy smile, and my thoughts reached back almost 20 years to my grandparents on our farm in KwaZulu Natal telling me stories of these very horses. The wild horses of what was then South West Africa, in the Namib desert. Stories that were probably somewhat romanticised. But what would you expect when their origin is "steeped in mystery" it is said. Since that time, it had been my dream to find them. And here I was.

My grandfather was of Irish descent and a great horseman. From him I have my love of horses as well as my horsemanship, such as it is. He has long since passed away and sadly the farm was sold along with our beloved horses. But he left me stories, memories, knowledge and an intense passion and love for these powerfully elegant animals. The legacy took hold of me and has lived and grown in my heart ever since. And perhaps it was my childhood years in semi-wilderness that have led me to believe that I can sometimes hear the call of the wild.

I wanted to know more, but at that time I was oblivious of the fact that another lover of horses had spent many years of field research working on a doctorate about the wild horses of Garub – the very animals I was seeking out in the Namib. Nor did I know that this learned lady, Telané Greyling, had joined forces with fellow horse-lover Mannfred Goldbeck, an enthusiast who had researched and documented all the explanations of the horses' origins, and that the result was a splendid book *Wild Horses of the Namib Desert*, an "equine biography" told by Ron Swilling. In the book, the authors strive to uncover all the secrets about these animals, their provenance, their

My grandfather on one of his beloved horses, Shamrock, at our family farm in KwaZulu Natal in the 1940s.

extraordinary powers of survival, their adaptation to a cruelly unwelcoming environment, their behaviour. They have greatly inspired me and encouraged me to strive to capture something of their essence through the lens of my camera, and I owe most of my insights to them.

Well into adulthood and after graduating in photography and design, I would still find my grandparents' tales and stories floating back into my dreams. Dreams of hard sun in my eyes, golden dust and glimpses of pounding hooves and long, swishing tails. I started having vivid visual images of animals I have never seen, and they invaded my dreams. The day came that I knew I had simply pack up and go.

Waking up one morning to a resolve that had been shaped in my dreams, I traded in my VW Polo for a small pick-up truck, bought a chunk of foam mattress cut to fit in the back of this bakkie, and packed my camping gear and my camera.

"Only three weeks, Mom," I said. I will never forget the words of my mother's life partner (who grew up in Namibia) when he leaned through the window to say goodbye on the morning of my departure: "Remember – the nothing grows very high there."

So I headed north with little more than a map of Namibia and no idea precisely where I was headed. I overnighted in a safari base camp on the banks of the Orange River where I had a view deep into Namibia on the far side, my heart racing at what I sensed awaited me there. The camp belonged to an old friend, a safari guide who's planted his tracks all over Africa for more than 15 years. I flattened my map on his bar counter, handed him a pen and asked him to draw me the route to the horses. He obliged, adding an obligatory stop at a place called Beta, home to "the best apple pie on the continent," he assured me.

I was to spend some weeks sleeping in the back of my bakkie under a thorn tree below the breathtaking dome of overcountable stars in a black sky. Supper made on my campfire consisted mainly of sweet potato (sometimes the only fresh veggies available in the desert) and whatever meat I could get from the local farmers. Breakfast I had to share with hundreds of Sociable

weavers – by the time I had fetched milk from my cooler, I would find nothing but a few crumbs left of my muesli. Their fear of humans was trumped by their need make the best of a free meal in the desert, which I suppose is how the fittest survive. Before sunrise I would be following the horses because by 8 am the heat was so severe I was forced to retreat to the shade of my acacia tree. With some field mice and lizards to keep me company until the late afternoon when the cool breeze meant I could follow the horses once again until after dark.

It was during those days that I lived my dream through the lens of my camera, an eye that sees what the mind has imagined and, if you get it right, captures it. In these pages I offer some of the images that made my spirit soar.

These Sociable weaver birds were constantly on the lookout for food and became accustomed enough to my presence to swoop down and sit in my hand in the hope of a crumb or two.

Gondwana Lodge

I camped alone off the road leading to Klein-Aus Vista, the Gondwana lodge closest to the area that the horses frequent, and saw only the occasional tourist passing through.

My magical time alone with the horses came to an end as the rainy season slowly made its way south. Again, I took the long road north. Driving through heavy rains on gravel roads where sometimes you wouldn't encounter another soul for days, there were times when I thought I would be stranded, or worse – upended, as the rain, mud and eroded roads time and again had me slithering towards disaster. Somewhere along the by now all but impassable route I met some 'bush pilots' who offered me a room to rent and hands to try and salvage my bakkie. By a combination of sheer luck and willpower we got my pick-up (and me) to Windhoek, the capital of Namibia. I was then prepared to vouch that my bakkie had the heart of a Toyota Landcruiser!

What is there to say about the horses after the superb book by Goldbeck and Greyling? I am neither a poet nor a scientist, but see myself as an artist – my camera my brush and canvas, the light my paint. I offer to you my journey, my interpretation, my passion through my photography.

Briefly, then, with grateful acknowledgement to the authors of *Wild Horses in the Namib Desert: an equine biography*, here is a little about the horses of Garub. Even to Greyling and Goldbeck, there remains much that is impenetrable. It's hard to say exactly how these horses ended up in such an

inhospitable place. Locals will tell of a shipwreck off the coast of Lüderitz from which the horses broke free and swam to their survival; other stories tell of the man who owned the Schloss Duwisib and went to fight in the war, never to return. His widowed wife, overcome with sorrow, cast open the gates and chased the horses into the desert. She returned to Europe and left the castle deserted.

It is also believed that when the First World War ended, cavalry abandoned their horses to fend for themselves in the desert. Simultaneously with these events, motor cars became part of the scene and many people simply let their horses go.

Research offers a more logical explanation of their origin. From 1909 to 1920, the mayor of Lüderitzbucht had a stud farm at Kubub near Garub, very close to where the horses still live today. It is believed that he abandoned his horses after losing all his wealth in the depression years. The horses were not constrained by fences and must have moved on to better grazing and water sources in the Garub area.

Along with the stud farm group, abandoned Shutztruppe (colonial German mounted troops) and settlers' horses, and railway workers horses, are all believed to have formed a herd.

When the Lüderitz railway was still operative, the horses would get water from the way stations. This area of Namibia is well known for its extreme weather conditions, mercilessly hot summers, with droughts that can last years, and bitterly cold winters – some years even snow. Given the enforced isolation of living in a restricted diamond area dubbed *Sperrgebiet* by the German colonists, there was protection from hunters with their only natural enemy being spotted hyenas, which mainly take out the sick and the young.

With the discontinuation of the railway, the need for water for the trains also dried up. Apart from a few water troughs, the source that waters the horses today was built in late 1991, a borehole drilled by local farmers. The waterhole is also frequented by the free-roaming game in the area, like gemsbok (oryx), jackal, hyena, kudu and other denizens of the desert.

Goldbeck and Greyling tell of the horses' inventive adaptation to their nutrition-poor environment. There is some grass, yes, as well as scattered shrubs and herbs. But in a triumph of the concept of recycling, these horses also consume their own manure. As horses don't digest cellulose as effectively as ruminants such as cattle, they gain high-energy food from their nutrient-rich manure. They are shaped into a social structure appropriate to their living conditions, consisting of breeding groups and bachelor stallions, with a fair amount of dispersal and exchange between breeding groups occurring. Among the various other features described by our two writers are leadership, competitive behaviour, breeding behaviour and co-operative

activity. They give a fascinating description of body language, including their posturing, greeting ritual, and their extraordinary dung-pile ritual accompanied by sniffing, squeals and displays of strength.

Combat occurs, but so too does playful behaviour and signals informing an approaching horse how welcome or otherwise his attentions are.

The authors conclude with reflections on the future of these herds, and means of doing justice to their high cultural and historical importance and their present-day value as a tourist attraction. I stand in awe of the dedication that went into decades of monitoring and studying these tough, extraordinarily well-adapted animals.

My few weeks in the desert might pale into insignificance by comparison, but those days have left me with memories to last a lifetime. My contribution is to offer my pictures in the hope that an inkling of the profound joy I found in the experience will come through in these images.

I went on a journey, but as time passes and the reflection continues, it becomes more mystical with every passing day.

Miona Janeke
Windhoek, November 2014

Every day I would go to the waterhole to wait for the horses to come and drink. When they saw the water they would break into a gallop – even the pregnant mare in the centre of the picture – vying with each other to be first to quench their thirst.

In the summer, Etosha National Park is bone dry. When the rains come, everything comes to life and the animals gratefully quench their thirst at the watering holes and puddles in the road. Travelling north one day, I saw a small speck across the Etosha salt pan. As the speck jogged toward my vehicle, I stopped, but I still couldn't see much for the brightness of the white sand. Eventually, I made out the shape of a cheetah, my first sighting of one in the wild. What an icon of freedom.

The Spitzkoppe

The Spitzkoppe is a Mecca for every rock climber and one of the most memorable places I have been. Camping with only a longdrop toilet surrounded by a simple reed wall, I certainly had a loo with a view!

The bushmen rock paintings, the crystals, the magnificent views from the peaks, and sleeping under a dome of brilliant stars contributed to making it a magical experience.

The herds vary in size and structure – from small bachelor herds to bigger ones with one or two breeding stallions as leaders. Although confllicts do occur when a stallion tries to muscle in where he's not wanted, real fights are rare – it's too hot and too tiring for that.

This sequence of photographs captured a confrontation between two stallions, as the light-maned stallion fended off a rival's designs on his mares.

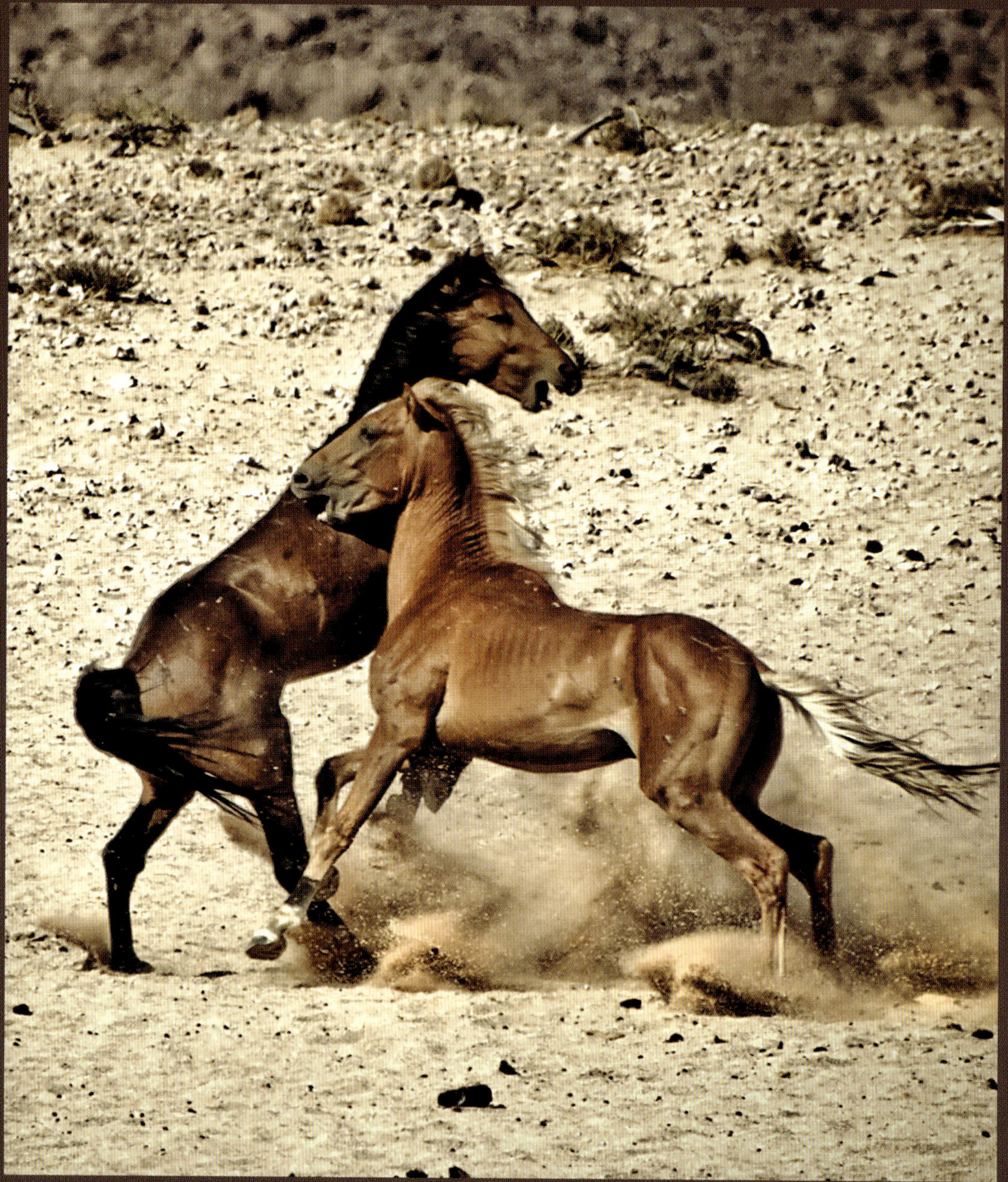

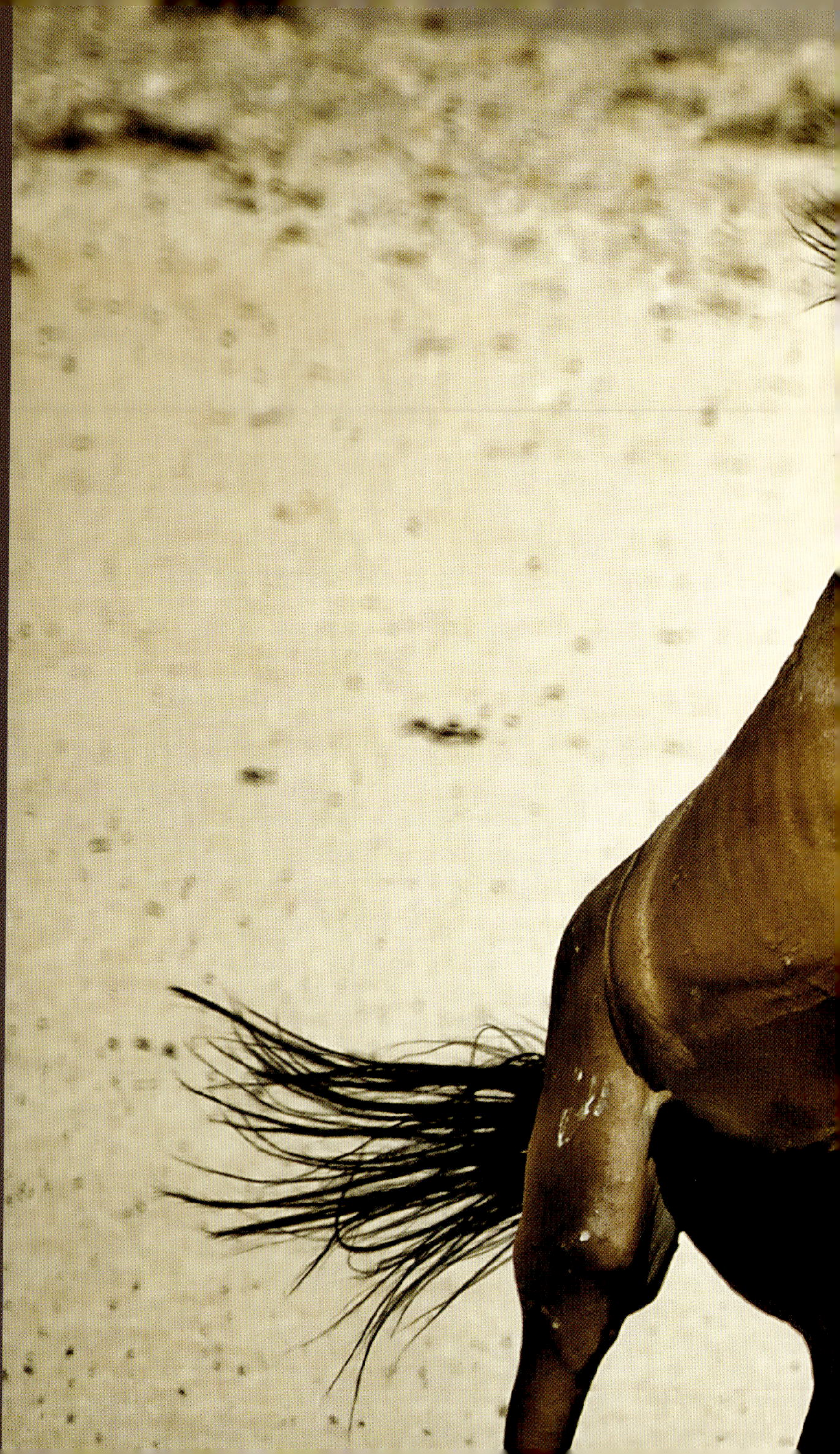

My straw hat became an ice-breaker in my relationship with the horses. Some of the young horses were very curious about it and came closer to investigate. When it blew off one day, these young colts thought it was lunch!

Sociable weaver birds build huge community nests that can fill a whole tree. I would watch them for hours as they flew in and out of their haystack-like home, wondering how they knew whose entrance was whose.

Below: while hiking one day, I came across the remains of an Orxy leg, a stark reminder of how harsh life in the desert can be.

Opposite: I was told that this bullet-riddled skeleton near Klein-Aus Vista had belonged to diamond thieves back in the day. They tried to make a run from the cops, thinking they would escape through a canyon – only to discover that it was a blind canyon. The police opened fire, the car was set alight and burnt the thieves with it – so the story goes.